A Year to Re

1944

For Those Whose Hearts Belong to 1944

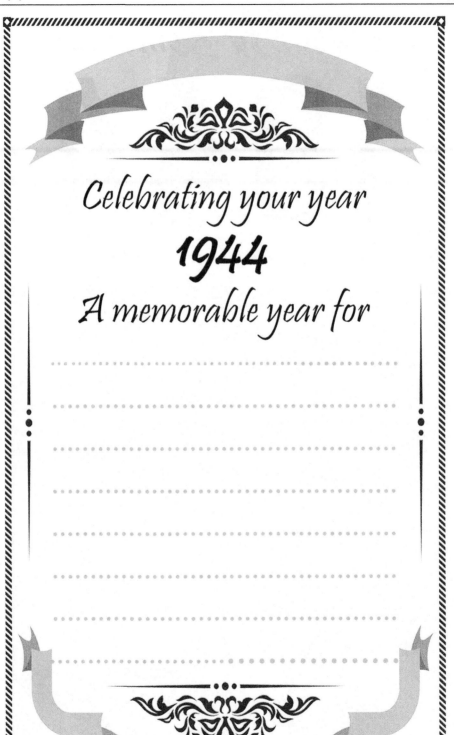

Celebrating your year
1944
A memorable year for

Contents
Introduction: A Glimpse into 1944

Chapter 5: Fashion, and Popular Leisure Activities

Chapter 6: Technological Advancements and Popular Cars

Chapter 7: Stats and the Cost of Things

Chapter 8: Iconic Advertisements of 1944

Introduction

A Year to Remember - 1944

For Those Whose Hearts Belong to 1944

To our cherished readers who hold a special connection to the year 1944, whether it's because you were born in this remarkable year, celebrated a milestone, or hold dear memories from that time, this book is a tribute to you and your unique connection to an unforgettable era.

In the pages that follow, we invite you to embark on a captivating journey back to 1944, a year of profound historical significance. For those with a personal connection to this year, it holds a treasure trove of memories, stories, and experiences that shaped the world and touched your lives.

Throughout this book, we've woven together the tapestry of 1944, providing historical insights, personal stories, and interactive activities that allow you to relive and celebrate the significance of this special year.

As you turn the pages and immerse yourself in the events and culture of 1944, we hope you'll find moments of nostalgia, inspiration, and the opportunity to rekindle cherished memories of this extraordinary year.

This book is dedicated to you, our readers, who share a unique bond with 1944. May it bring you joy, enlightenment, and a deeper connection to the rich tapestry of history that weaves through your lives.

With warm regards,

Edwardlab.com

Chapter 1:
Politics and Leading Events around the World

1.1 The Global Stage in 1944: Where Were You?
France D-Day

On June 6,1944, Operation Overlord, code named D-Day, more than 156,000 American, British and Canadian troops stormed 50 miles of Normandy's fiercely defended beaches in northern France in an operation that prove to be a critical turning point in World War II

D-Day landings: June 6, 1944

Liberation of Paris (August 25, 1944):

Allied forces, including the Free French forces under General Charles de Gaulle, liberated the city of Paris from German occupation. This event was a symbol of hope and marked a turning point in the war in Western Europe.

Paris is liberated from Nazi occupation August 25

Siege of Leningrad Broken

1. The Siege of Leningrad (St. Petersburg) ends on January 27 News Events of 1944.

2. The siege began on September 8th of 1941 when the city was surrounded by German and Finnish troops.

3. The city was blockaded and roads and trains were cut off. Leningrad was defended by about 200,000 Soviet troops.

4. Nazi Germany targeted Leningrad for its symbolic significance as the home of the Russian Revolution as well as its strategic significance as a manufacturing hub for the Soviet Union.

5. Over one million people died, primarily from starvation, and it turned into one of the longest and most devastating sieges in history.

6. It was finally broken after 872 days.

Philippines Battle of Leyte Gulf

The Battle of Leyte Gulf takes place during the month of October . The main battle took place between October 23rd and 26th and was considered one of the largest naval battles in world history. United States, Australian, and Filipino forces began the invasion of Japanese occupied Philippines by landing in the Leyte Gulf. The Japanese suffered heavy losses to their navy and it marked their first kamikaze aerial attacks. The Allies won the battle and their victory lead to the liberation of the Philippines. This was a turning point in the war against Japan as it effectively cut off their supply route in Southeast Asia and was a devastating loss to their naval forces with many of their ships destroyed and thousands killed.

Iceland -- Independence

The Republic of Iceland is founded during February. The Icelandic parliament decided to sever ties between Iceland and Denmark and proposed a referendum to determine the nation's future. The referendum was held in May of that year and citizens overwhelmingly voted in favor of severing ties with Denmark and established a republic. There was 98 percent turnout and over 90 percent voted in favor of both criteria. The country's official celebration of independence came in June when the republic was formally created and its first president, Sveinn Bjornsson, took office.

1.2 Leaders and Statesmen: Movers and Shakers of '44

As we delve into the year 1944, it's important to recognize the key leaders and statesmen who played pivotal roles in shaping the course of history during this challenging period.

President Franklin D. Roosevelt: America's Steady Hand

At the forefront of global affairs was President Franklin D. Roosevelt. In 1944, Roosevelt was in the midst of his fourth term as the President of the United States. He was a remarkable leader known for his calm and resolute demeanor during wartime. Roosevelt worked tirelessly to coordinate Allied efforts in both the European and Pacific theaters of World War II. His leadership was instrumental in guiding the United States and its allies through this tumultuous period.

Winston Churchill: The Bulldog Spirit of Britain

Across the Atlantic, British Prime Minister Winston Churchill was a stalwart figure. Churchill's leadership and unwavering resolve inspired the British people during their darkest hours. He worked closely with Roosevelt and other Allied leaders to develop strategies to defeat Nazi Germany. Churchill's speeches, filled with determination and eloquence, remain iconic symbols of British resilience.

Joseph Stalin: The Soviet Bear

On the Eastern Front, Soviet Premier Joseph Stalin was a force to be reckoned with. Stalin's leadership was instrumental in the Soviet Union's ability to withstand the brutal onslaught of Nazi forces. Under his command, the Red Army mounted a fierce resistance, ultimately turning the tide of the war in favor of the Allies. Stalin's strategic prowess and determination were crucial factors in the defeat of Nazi Germany.

Adolf Hitler: The Face of the Axis Powers

On the opposing side, Adolf Hitler continued to lead Nazi Germany in 1944. Despite the mounting losses and setbacks, Hitler remained a formidable figure. Nazi Germany was deeply entrenched in the war effort, and Hitler's leadership style was marked by authoritarianism and aggression. However, by 1944, the tide of the conflict had begun to turn against the Axis Powers.

General Charles de Gaulle: The Free French Leader

General Charles de Gaulle emerged as a symbol of hope for the French people. Leading the Free French forces, he tirelessly worked to liberate France from German occupation. The liberation of Paris on August 25, 1944, was a momentous occasion, and de Gaulle's return to the city marked the beginning of the end for the Nazi regime in France.

Activity:
Historical Crossword
Test Your Knowledge of '44

Are you ready to challenge your knowledge of the significant events and key figures of 1944? Here's a crossword puzzle that will test your understanding of the historic year.

ACROSS

4. Operation Overlord, a critical turning point in World War II

5. The longest and most devastating siege in history finally ended in this city on January 27, 1944

7. The Republic of this country was founded in February 1944, severing ties with Denmark

8. Nazi leader who continued to lead Germany in 1944

9. Soviet Premier who led the Red Army to victory against Nazi forces

DOWN

1. Allied forces liberated this city from German occupation on August 25, 1944

2. British Prime Minister known for his speeches of determination

3. General who became a symbol of hope for the Free French forces

5. One of the largest naval battles in history took place in this gulf during October 1944

6. President of the United States during World War II

Enjoy the journey into history!

Chapter 2:
The Iconic Movies, TV Shows, and Awards

2.1 Memorable Films of '44

Double Indemnity: Directed by Billy Wilder, this film is a classic example of film noir.
It features Fred MacMurray as an insurance salesman and Barbara Stanwyck as a femme fatale, leading to a web of deception and murder.

Going My Way: Directed by Leo McCarey and starring Bing Crosby as Father Chuck O'Malley, this heartwarming film tells the story of a priest who uses his unconventional methods to connect with a struggling New York parish.

Meet Me in St. Louis:

Directed by Vincente Minnelli and starring Judy Garland, this musical film is set against the backdrop of the 1904 World's Fair in St. Louis. It features the beloved song "The Trolley Song" and captures the essence of American life at the turn of the century.

Laura:

Directed by Otto Preminger, "Laura" is a stylish film noir that weaves a tale of mystery and obsession. The film's haunting score and cinematography, along with Gene Tierney's captivating performance as the titular character, make it a classic in the noir genre.

Gaslight:

Directed by George Cukor, "Gaslight" stars Ingrid Bergman as Paula Alquist Anton, a woman who believes she's going insane in her own home. Charles Boyer's sinister portrayal of her husband adds to the suspense and drama.

2.2 TV Shows That Captivated the Nation

While television was still in its infancy in 1944, a few note-worthy programs emerged to captivate audiences and pave the way for the future of television entertainment. Here are some TV shows from 1944 that captured the nation's attention:

The Voice of Firestone:

This was one of the earliest musical television programs. "The Voice of Firestone" originated as a radio program but made its television debut in 1944. It featured classical music performances, often with opera singers, and was sponsored by the Firestone Tire and Rubber Company. The show was significant in the early history of televised musical performances.

The Edgar Bergen and Charlie McCarthy Show:

Edgar Bergen was a ventriloquist, and Charlie McCarthy was his famous puppet. This radio show made its transition to television in 1944, becoming one of the earliest examples of a ventriloquist act adapted for TV. The show was a comedy variety program and became quite popular, paving the way for future ventriloquist acts on television.

2.3 Prestigious Film Awards and Honors

In 1944, despite the challenges posed by World War II, the film industry continued to recognize excellence through prestigious awards and honors. Here are some notable film awards and honors from that year:

Academy Awards (Oscars):

Best Picture: "Casablanca"

Best Director: Michael Curtiz for "Casablanca"

Best Actor: Paul Lukas for "Watch on the Rhine"

Best Actress: Jennifer Jones for "The Song of Bernadette"

Best Supporting Actor: Charles Coburn for "The More the Merrier"

Best Supporting Actress: Katina Paxinou for "For Whom the Bell Tolls"

Cannes Film Festival:

While the Cannes Film Festival was not held during the war years (1940-1945), it would resume in 1946. However, it's important to note that this prestigious festival would play a significant role in recognizing and promoting international cinema in the post-war era.

2.4. Entertainment That Shaped the Era

In the year 1944, amidst the backdrop of World War II, entertainment played a crucial role in shaping the cultural landscape and providing solace and diversion to people around the world. Here's a closer look at how entertainment influenced and reflected the era:

1. Film: A Source of Escapism

Movies in 1944 were not just a form of entertainment but also a means of escape from the harsh realities of the war. Classics like "Casablanca" and "Double Indemnity" transported audiences to worlds of intrigue, romance, and suspense, offering a temporary respite from the global conflict.

2. Radio: The Pulse of Information

Radio broadcasts continued to be a primary source of news and entertainment. Radio dramas, comedy shows, and music programs not only entertained but also informed the public about the progress of the war. Programs like "The Edgar Bergen and Charlie McCarthy Show" brought humor into living rooms.

3. Literature: Escapism and Reflection

Books and literature offered an avenue for both escapism and reflection. Authors like Agatha Christie and George Orwell penned novels that resonated with readers, providing mystery and social commentary. People turned to literature as a means of intellectual engagement amid the chaos.

4. Television: An Emerging Medium

Television was still in its early stages, but programs like "The Voice of Firestone" and "The Edgar Bergen and Charlie McCarthy Show" marked the beginning of televised entertainment, foreshadowing the role television would play in shaping future cultures.

Activity:
Movie and TV Show Trivia Quiz

How Well Do You Know '44 Entertainment?

Instructions: Read the questions and select the correct answers by marking the corresponding letter (A, B, C, or D)

Question 1: In 1944, which classic film directed by Billy Wilder featured Fred MacMurray as an insurance salesman and Barbara Stanwyck as a femme fatale?

A) Casablanca

B) Double Indemnity

C) Laura

D) Gaslight

Question 2: Who starred as Father Chuck O'Malley in the heartwarming film "Going My Way," directed by Leo McCarey?

A) Humphrey Bogart

B) Bing Crosby

C) Fred Astaire

D) Cary Grant

Question 3: "Meet Me in St. Louis," set against the backdrop of the 1904 World's Fair, featured the beloved song "The Trolley Song." Who played the lead role in this musical film?

A) Judy Garland

B) Marilyn Monroe

C) Audrey Hepburn

D) Grace Kelly

Question 4: Which film directed by Otto Preminger in 1944 is considered a classic in the film noir genre and tells a tale of mystery and obsession?

A) Laura

B) Double Indemnity

C) Casablanca

D) The Maltese Falcon

Question 5: In the film "Gaslight," directed by George Cukor, who played the role of Paula Alquist Anton, a woman who believes she's going insane in her own home?

A) Ingrid Bergman

B) Barbara Stanwyck

C) Lauren Bacall

D) Vivien Leigh

Question 6: "The Voice of Firestone" was one of the earliest musical television programs in 1944. What type of music performances did it feature?

A) Jazz music

B) Rock and roll music

C) Classical music performances

D) Country music

Question 7: Edgar Bergen and his famous puppet, Charlie McCarthy, made the transition from radio to television in 1944. What type of program was "The Edgar Bergen and Charlie McCarthy Show"?

A) Cooking show

B) News program

C) Variety show

D) Travel documentary

Question 8: In 1944, which film won the Academy Award for Best Picture, becoming one of the most iconic films of all time?

A) Double Indemnity

B) Laura

C) Casablanca

D) Gone with the Wind

Question 9: The Cannes Film Festival was not held during the war years but would resume in 1946. True or False?

A) True

B) False

Question 10: In 1944, which emerging medium began to pave the way for future televised entertainment, featuring programs like "The Voice of Firestone" and "The Edgar Bergen and Charlie McCarthy Show"?

A) Radio

B) Internet

C) Television

D) Theater

Chapter 3:
Music: Top Songs, Albums, and Awards

3.1 Chart-Toppers and Musical Trends

Step back in time to the year 1944, a pivotal period in history marked by the ongoing turmoil of World War II. Despite the global unrest, the world of music continued to thrive, offering a respite and a source of comfort to people worldwide. In this musical time capsule, we'll explore the chart-toppers and prevailing musical trends of 1944.

Chart-Toppers of 1944:

"Swinging on a Star" & "I'll Be Seeing You" by Bing Crosby

"The Trolley Song" is a song featured in the 1944 film Meet
Me in St. Louis sung by Judy Garland as Esther Smith

Musical Trends of 1944:

1944 was a year marked by musical diversity and resilience
in the face of wartime challenges. Swing music, sentimental ballads, crooning, and film music continued to captivate
audiences, offering both entertainment and emotional connection during a tumultuous period in history. These musical trends provide a window into the cultural and emotional
landscape of the time.

1. Swing Music:

Swing music continued to dominate the airwaves, with big band leaders like Glenn Miller, Benny Goodman, Tommy Dorsey, and Duke Ellington captivating audiences with their infectious rhythms and spirited performances. Swing offered a lively and uplifting soundtrack to wartime America.

2. Sentimental Ballads:

Sentimental ballads held a special place in the hearts of listeners. These emotional and often romantic songs provided comfort and solace, allowing people to express their feelings and longings during the war's separations and uncertainties.

3. Crooning:

Crooners like Bing Crosby and Frank Sinatra gained immense popularity. Their smooth and intimate vocal styles resonated with audiences, offering a sense of intimacy and connection through their music.

4. Film Music:

Film music played a significant role in the music industry, with iconic movie songs like "The Trolley Song" and "I'll Be Seeing You" becoming chart-toppers. Movie soundtracks provided an emotional and cultural bridge between the cinema and the music scene.

5. Patriotic Songs:

Patriotic songs continued to inspire a sense of national unity and pride. Songs like "This Land Is Your Land" by Woody Guthrie and "Praise the Lord and Pass the Ammunition" by Kay Kyser conveyed messages of resilience and determination.

6. Vocal Harmony Groups:

Vocal harmony groups, such as The Andrews Sisters, brought a sense of camaraderie and joy with their upbeat performances. Their close harmonies and catchy tunes resonated with a wide audience.

7. Jazz and Bebop:

Jazz continued to evolve, with the emergence of bebop introducing complex melodies and improvisation. Artists like Dizzy Gillespie and Charlie Parker pushed the boundaries of jazz, paving the way for future musical innovations.

3.2 Music Awards and Honors

Academy Awards (Oscars) for Best Original Song (1944): "Swinging on a Star" - Music by Jimmy Van Heusen, Lyrics by Johnny Burke

The Billboard No. 1 song of 1944: "I'll Be Seeing You" by Bing Crosby

Top Selling Singles of 1944 (USA)

"I'll Be Seeing You" by Bing Crosby

"Swinging on a Star" by Bing Crosby

"Don't Fence Me In" by Bing Crosby and The Andrews Sisters

"Mairzy Doats" by The Merry Macs

Activity: Music Lyrics Challenge

Guess the Song Lyrics from '44

Introduction: Test your knowledge of 1944's music by completing these song lyrics from that era. Can you identify the songs and the artists behind them? Fill in the missing words!

1. "Would you like to _____ on a star? Carry _____ _____ home in a _____. And be better off than you are?"

2. "I'll be _____ you in all the _____ places that keep us out of _____."

3. "Clang, clang, clang went the _____. Ding, ding, ding went the _____."

4. "This land is your land, this land is my land, from California to the New York _____."

5. "Praise the Lord and pass the _____. Praise the Lord and pass the _____."

6. "Don't fence me in. Let me be by _____ in the _____ under the western _____."

7. "Mairzy doats and dozy doats and liddle lamzy divey. A _____ of _____, a liddle _____ too. Wouldn't you?"

Enjoy this musical journey back to 1944, and see how well you can recall these memorable song lyrics from that era!

Chapter 4: Sports in 1944

In 1944, Sporting achievements and memorable victories were notable despite the ongoing challenges of World War II. Sports served as a source of inspiration and unity during these turbulent times. Here are some of the key athletic achievements and memorable victories from 1944:

4.1 Sporting achievements and Memorable Victories

Olympic Games Canceled:

The Summer and Winter Olympic Games scheduled for 1944 were canceled due to World War II. Many athletes from around the world were involved in military service or supporting the war effort. The cancellation marked a somber period for the sporting world.

PGA Championship Men's Golf, Manito G & CC:

Bob Hamilton wins his only major title, 1 up in the 36-hole final over heavily favoured Byron Nelson

Golfer
Bob Hamilton

US National Championships:

American Frank Parker wins 1st of 4 Grand Slam titles; beats William Talbert 6-4, 3-6, 6-3, 6-3

Pauline Betz Addie wins her third straight US title; beats Margaret Osborne 6-3, 8-6

Boston Marathon:

In the 48th Boston Marathon, Gerard Cote of Canada secured his second consecutive victory, marking his third out of four total titles, with a remarkable finishing time of 2 hours, 31 minutes, and 50.4 seconds.

4.2 American Sports: Champions and Championship Moments
Baseball's World Series:

The St. Louis Cardinals faced off against the St. Louis Browns in the 1944 World Series. The Cardinals emerged victorious, winning their fifth World Series title.

Baseball record:

On April 30th, Mel Ott of the New York Giants made base-ball history by scoring 6 runs in one game while drawing 5 walks. This remarkable feat highlighted his exceptional skills on the field.

Chicago Cubs and Baseball History:

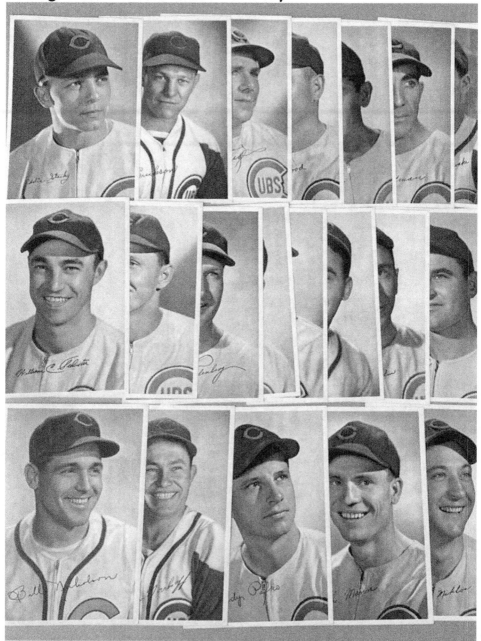

The Chicago Cubs set a major league record in 1944 by playing in their 62nd and final consecutive home game without committing an error. This achievement remains a notable chapter in baseball history.

NFL Championship:

National Football League Championship, Polo Grounds, NYC: Green Bay Packers beat New York Giants, 14-7 for 6th and final league title under long-time coach Curly Lambeau.

The New York Rangers' Stanley Cup Victory:

1943   **New York Rangers**   1944

The New York Rangers, an NHL team, captured the Stanley Cup in 1944. This victory was particularly special as it ended a long championship drought for the Rangers.

48th Boston Marathon won by Gerard Cote of Canada in 2:31:50.4; second straight victory; 3rd of 4 titles

NHL history:

Dec 28 Montreal right wing Maurice 'Rocket' Richard becomes first player in NHL history to score 8 points in one game with 5 goals and 3 assists in the Canadiens' 9-1 win over the Detroit Red Wings

Activity:
Sports Trivia - Test Your Knowledge of 1944 Sports History

Instructions: Read the questions and select the correct answers by marking the corresponding letter (A, B, C, or D).

1. Which major sporting event was canceled in 1944 due to World War II?

a) Super Bowl

b) FIFA World Cup

c) Olympic Games

d) Wimbledon

2. Who won the PGA Championship in men's golf in 1944, defeating the heavily favored Byron Nelson?

a) Arnold Palmer

b) Jack Nicklaus

c) Bob Hamilton

d) Ben Hogan

3. In the US National Championships, which American tennis player won his first of four Grand Slam titles in 1944?

a) John McEnroe

b) Pete Sampras

c) Andre Agassi

d) Frank Parker

4. Who secured her third consecutive US title in women's tennis by defeating Margaret Osborne in 1944?

a) Serena Williams

b) Maria Sharapova

c) Venus Williams

d) Pauline Betz Addie

5. Which MLB team won the 1944 World Series?
a) New York Yankees
b) Brooklyn Dodgers
c) St. Louis Cardinals
d) Boston Red Sox

6. In baseball, who set a record in 1944 by scoring 6 runs in one game while drawing 5 walks?
a) Babe Ruth
b) Lou Gehrig
c) Mel Ott
d) Ty Cobb

7. What major league baseball record did the Chicago Cubs set in 1944?
a) Consecutive no-hitters
b) Most home runs in a season
c) Most consecutive errorless home games
d) Longest winning streak

8. Which NHL team won the Stanley Cup in 1944, ending a long championship drought?
a) Montreal Canadiens
b) Toronto Maple Leafs
c) New York Rangers
d) Detroit Red Wings

9. Who became the first player in NHL history to score 8 points in one game with 5 goals and 3 assists in 1944?
a) Wayne Gretzky
b) Bobby Orr
c) Gordie Howe
d) Maurice 'Rocket' Richard

10. What was the finishing time of Gerard Cote in the 1944 Boston Marathon, where he secured his second consecutive victory?
a) 2 hours, 10 minutes, and 30 seconds
b) 2 hours, 31 minutes, and 50.4 seconds
c) 3 hours, 15 minutes, and 40 seconds
d) 2 hours, 45 minutes, and 20.2 seconds

Chapter 5:
Fashion, and Popular Leisure Activities

5.1 Fashion Flashback: What the World Wore in '44

In 1944, the world of fashion was influenced by the ongoing events of World War II. While the war had a significant impact on clothing and fashion choices, people still found ways to express their style and individuality. Here's a glimpse of what the world wore in '44:

1. Utility Clothing:

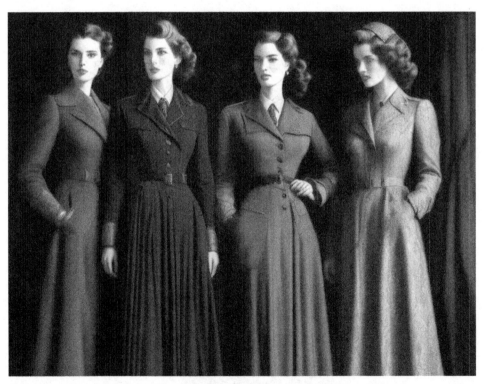

Due to wartime rationing and the need to conserve resources, utility clothing became prevalent. These garments were designed to be practical and functional, with minimal use of fabric and embellishments. Utility dresses and suits were often characterized by simple lines and practical features.

2. Military Influence:

Military-inspired fashion was in vogue, with elements like epaulets, brass buttons, and trench coats being popular choices. Women's fashion saw the adaptation of military-style jackets and pants, reflecting the spirit of solidarity and patriotism.

3. Victory Suits:

Victory suits were tailored outfits for women that featured straight skirts, short jackets, and padded shoulders. These suits symbolized the strength and resilience of women during the war years.

4. Headscarves:

Headscarves became a fashionable accessory, not only as a style statement but also as a practical way to protect hairstyles during air raids. Women would tie colorful scarves around their heads, adding a touch of flair to their wartime attire.

5. Zoot Suits:

In contrast to the utilitarian clothing of the era, zoot suits emerged as a rebellious and flamboyant fashion trend among young men, particularly in the United States. Zoot suits featured oversized jackets with wide shoulders and baggy trousers with cuffs. These suits were often worn with fedora hats and pointed shoes.

6. Wedge Shoes:

High heels were in short supply due to wartime restrictions on materials, so wedge shoes became a popular alternative. Wedges offered both style and comfort, making them a practical choice for women.

7. Berets and Turbans:

Berets and turbans were fashionable headwear choices for women. They added an air of sophistication and elegance to outfits while also keeping hair neatly in place.

8. Red Lipstick:

Red lipstick became a symbol of resilience and glamour during the war. Women often wore bright red lipstick to boost their morale and maintain a sense of femininity.

9. Practical Handbags:

Handbags were designed with practicality in mind. Many featured multiple compartments and secure closures to accommodate rationing coupons, identification, and other essentials.

5.2 Entertainment and Hobbies

In 1944, amid the backdrop of World War II, people around the world sought out leisure pursuits and hobbies that provided solace, distraction, and a sense of normalcy in tumultuous times. Here's a glimpse into the leisure activities and hobbies that were popular in 1944:

1.Radio Entertainment:

Radio remained a central source of entertainment and information. Families gathered around the radio to listen to comedy shows, music broadcasts, news updates, and thrilling dramas. Popular programs like "The Edgar Bergen and Charlie McCarthy Show" brought humor into homes.

2.Reading and Literature:

Books and magazines offered an escape from the realities of war. Novels by authors such as Agatha Christie, George Orwell, and Ernest Hemingway provided both entertainment and intellectual engagement. Reading was a cherished pastime.

Agatha Christie   George Orwell

3.Home Gardening:

Many people turned to home gardening as a productive and therapeutic hobby. Victory gardens, as they were known, allowed individuals to grow their own fruits and vegetables, contributing to food self-sufficiency and the war effort.

4.Letter Writing:

Letter writing took on great importance during the war. Soldiers and civilians exchanged heartfelt letters, offering comfort and maintaining connections across long distances. Correspondence was a lifeline for those separated by the conflict.

5.Board Games and Puzzles:

Board games and jigsaw puzzles provided indoor entertainment for families. Classics like Monopoly, Scrabble, and Clue offered hours of amusement and friendly competition, strengthening family bonds.

6.Sewing and Crafting:

Sewing, knitting, and crafting allowed individuals to express creativity and make practical items. Women often sewed clothing and accessories, while others engaged in knitting and crocheting projects.

7.Music and Dancing:

Music continued to be a source of joy and entertainment. Swing music and big band performances filled dance halls, offering a chance to let loose and enjoy life through dance and music.

8.Photography:

Photography enthusiasts captured moments of daily life and documented the war effort. Amateur photographers found solace in their hobby, creating visual records of wartime experiences.

9.Scrapbooking:

Scrapbooking gained popularity as a means of chronicling events, collecting mementos, and creating visual diaries. Scrapbooks often included newspaper clippings, photographs, and personal reflections, preserving memories for future generations.

Activity:
Fashion Design Coloring Page
Create Your 44-Inspired Outfit

Chapter 6:
Technological Advancements and Popular Cars

6.1 Innovations That Shaped the Future
1.Kidney Dialysis:

In 1944, a remarkable medical breakthrough occurred in the Netherlands with the invention of kidney dialysis by Dutch physician Willem Kolff. Dr. Kolff's pioneering work led to the development of the first practical dialysis machine, known as the "artificial kidney." This invention marked a significant turning point in the treatment of kidney failure and laid the foundation for modern renal medicine. Kidney dialysis became a lifesaving procedure, providing hope and extended life to countless individuals suffering from kidney-related illnesses. Dr. Kolff's innovation revolutionized healthcare, offering a new lease on life for those previously without effective treatment options

2.Sunscreen:

In 1944, American pharmacist Benjamin Green made a significant contribution to skincare and sun protection with the invention of a groundbreaking product – sunscreen. Recognizing the need to protect soldiers in the Pacific Theater of World War II from the harsh sun, Green developed a substance known as "Red Vet Pet" (Red Veterinary Petrolatum). This petroleum-based ointment acted as an effective barrier against the sun's harmful ultraviolet (UV) rays, preventing sunburn and skin damage. Green's innovation marked the birth of modern sunscreen, and his pioneering work laid the foundation for the development of the sunscreen products we use today to shield our skin from the sun's harmful effects. His invention not only protected soldiers during the war but also revolutionized skincare and sun safety practices for generations to come.

Automatic Sequence Controlled Calculator:

IBM dedicated the Automatic Sequence Controlled Calculator (ASCC), better known as the Harvard Mark I, to Harvard University. Mark I was the largest electromechanical calculator ever built and the first automatic digital calculator in the United States at the time.

6.2 The Automobiles of '44

In 1944, due to the ongoing World War II and its impact on the automobile industry, there were limited options for new civilian vehicles. Most car manufacturers had shifted their production to support the war effort, and the availability of new cars was scarce. As a result, there were no notable "best" or new automobile models introduced in 1944.

Instead, the best cars of the era were those from the pre-war years, known for their reliability, classic styling, and durability. Some of the popular models from that time included:

Ford Deluxe:

The Ford Deluxe was known for its affordability and practicality, making it a popular choice among American consumers.

It typically featured a V8 engine, providing decent power and performance.

The car's design was sleek and iconic, with distinctive features such as the classic front grille and streamlined body.

Chevrolet Fleetmaster:

. Chevrolet's Fleetmaster series offered a comfortable and smooth ride.

. It was equipped with Chevrolet's reliable inline-six-cylinder engine, known for its durability and fuel efficiency.

. The Fleetmaster's design was characterized by a stylish front grille and fender-mounted headlights, giving it a classic look.

Buick Super:

. The Buick Super was renowned for its performance and luxury features.

. It often came with a powerful inline-eight-cylinder engine, delivering impressive horsepower and torque.

. The Super boasted a more upscale interior with comfortable seating and upscale amenities.

Plymouth Special Deluxe:

The Plymouth Special Deluxe was a dependable choice known for its reliability.

It typically featured a sturdy inline-six-cylinder engine, providing good fuel economy.

The car's design was practical and functional, with a spacious interior and straightforward styling.

Activity: Cars 1944 ~ Wordsearch

Find the names of popular car models from 1944 in the puzzle below. The words may be hidden horizontally, vertically, or diagonally, and they can be written forwards or backward.

```
F  E  K  Z  U  X  Y  N  W  F  V  R  A  G  Q
A  W  X  X  L  B  Y  Z  N  P  A  F  Q  N  V
U  S  O  G  B  U  I  C  K  S  U  P  E  R  K
M  H  T  H  J  P  V  S  X  R  B  O  K  U  F
B  Q  F  U  X  F  Z  Q  Y  F  J  V  P  B  L
W  C  O  G  C  A  X  O  X  L  C  Z  V  S  E
P  S  R  O  H  H  V  G  N  X  B  N  Y  C  E
J  X  D  K  E  U  S  K  F  W  P  Q  X  P  T
E  Z  D  G  M  G  O  W  I  V  J  G  Y  Y  M
Y  D  E  I  Z  R  M  S  K  X  X  T  F  C  A
B  I  L  P  L  Y  M  O  U  T  H  E  V  J  S
B  N  U  N  L  Q  I  C  U  Q  S  A  J  E  T
T  V  X  C  U  T  Y  E  X  G  T  I  A  B  E
N  Q  E  R  X  O  X  U  K  S  W  X  U  L  R
F  O  Q  Y  C  H  E  V  R  O  L  E  T  W  A
```

Enjoy the word search, and have fun discovering these classic car models from 1944!

Chapter 7: Stats and the Cost of Things

7.1 Cost of Living in 1944

Average Cost of new house $3,450.00

Average wages per year $2,400.00

Average Monthly Rent $50.00 per month

Cost of a gallon of Gas 15 cents

A first class stamp 3 cents

Steamship

Loaf of Bread 10 cents

Old Spice Shaving Soap $1.00

1944 Grocery Prices

Automobiles
NO NEW CARS ADVERTISED FOR SALE, WWII
Used, Oldsmobile, sedan, 1934, 50.00
Used, Packard, 120 sedan, 1936, 175.00

Clothing
Men's coat, worsted, 50.00-65.00/each
Men's suit, Stein Bloch, 50.00-60.00/each
Men's shoes, Nunn-Bush, 10.00-13.50/pair
Men's shirts, Van Heusen "lightweight," 2.50/each
Women's suit, cotton, 7.89/each
Women's dress, cotton and seersucker, 8.98-12.95/each
Women's handbags, 7.50-13.95/each
Infant's dresses, 1.79/each
Hats, 7.95/each

Food & beverages
Apples, Rome, .23/2 lbs
Bacon, sliced, Sunnyfield, .37/lb
Beans, baked, B & M, .10/13 oz can
Beef, pot roast, .27/lb
Bread, white, Marvel, .09/20.5 oz loaf
Butter, Louetta, .49/lb
Cereal, Kellogg's Corn Flakes, .08/11 oz package
Chicken, fryers, .48/lb
Coffee, Eight O'Clock brand, .41/2 lbs
Duck, Long Island, .35/lb
Cheese, American or Velveeta, Kraft, .21/half pound
Cookies, Fig Newtons, Nabisco, .15/7 oz package
Corn, canned, Niblets, .10/12 oz can
Crisco, .23/lb jar
Eggs, Grade A, .45/dozen
Fish, cod, fresh, .25/lb

Garden equipment

Garbage can, 9 gallon, .98/each

Hose, rubber, 25', 1.69-2.19/each

7.2 Inflation and Its Effects

In 1944, the United States experienced significant inflationary pressures due to the ongoing World War II. This inflation, while not hyperinflation, had notable effects on the U.S. economy and its citizens. Here's an overview of inflation and its effects in 1944

War-Driven Inflation:

One of the primary causes of inflation in 1944 was the massive government spending required to support the war effort. The U.S. government financed the war through a combination of increased taxes, borrowing, and printing money.

The war spending injected a substantial amount of currency into the economy, leading to rising prices for goods and services.

Price Controls and Rationing:

To combat inflation and ensure equitable distribution of essential goods, the U.S. government implemented price controls and rationing.

Price controls were designed to limit the increase in the cost of items like food, fuel, and housing, preventing rampant inflation in these areas.

Demand for Consumer Goods:

With millions of Americans employed in war-related industries, there was a surge in demand for consumer products. People working in these industries earned higher wages, increasing their purchasing power.

This heightened demand, coupled with wartime production restrictions, led to rising prices for everyday items.

Wage Increases:
To attract workers to essential war industries, wages saw substantial increases. This helped offset the financial challenges of rising prices for many households.
Workers in munitions factories, shipyards, and other critical sectors enjoyed improved incomes.

Resource Scarcity:
The war effort diverted critical resources such as rubber, gasoline, and metals to military use. This scarcity of resources for civilian production contributed to rising costs and prices.

Inflation's Impact on Consumers:
Inflation eroded the purchasing power of consumers, making it more challenging for families to afford basic necessities. Many had to adjust their spending habits and make sacrifices.
For those who had saved money before the war, inflation eroded the value of their savings.

Government Interventions:
The U.S. government implemented various measures to combat inflation, including the sale of war bonds to absorb excess currency from the economy.
These interventions aimed to stabilize prices and redirect resources toward the war effort.

Transition to Post-War Economy:
Inflation continued into the post-war period, leading to economic adjustments as the nation transitioned from a wartime to a peacetime economy.
The post-war years brought their own economic challenges, including the potential for post-war deflation.

Activity:
1944 Shopping List Challenge

Transport yourself back to 1944 and take on the role of a savvy home economist with this engaging activity. Your mission is to plan a delicious meal using the provided ingredients and calculate the total cost while adhering to wartime budget constraints.

Groceries:

Frying chickens: 55 cents/pound
Pork loins: 28 cents/pound
Short ribs: 17 cents/pound
Hamburger: 25 cents/pound
Bacon: 29 cents/pound
Fresh perch: 37 cents/pound
Mullet fillers 37 cents/pound
Baby pike: 59 cents/pound
Walleyed pike: 39 cents/pound
Eggs: 33 cents/dozen
Butter: 46 cents/pound
Orange: 25 cents/4 pounds
Grapefruit: 25 cents/4 pounds
Tomatoes: 23 cents/4 pounds
Radishes : 3 for 13 cents
Asparagus : 2 for 15 cents
Potatoes: 25 cents/5 pounds
Cabbage: 5 cents/pounds
Crytal White laundry soap: 14 cents/3 bars
Salts: 5 cents for 26 Oz drum
Peas: 10 cents for 20 Oz can

SHOPPING List

	Item	Price	# Units	Total Price
☐				
☐				
☐				
☐				
☐				
☐				
☐				
☐				
☐				
☐				
☐				
☐				
☐				
☐				
☐				
☐				
☐				
☐				
			Total	

This Challenge allows you to step into the shoes of a home cook during a time of economic challenges. It's an opportunity to explore culinary creativity while respecting historical budgetary limitations. Enjoy your meal, and reflect on the ingenuity of those who made do with what they had during wartime.

Chapter 8:
Iconic Advertisements of 1944

8.1 Remembering Vintage Ads
1944 Whitman Chocolates Classic Vintage Print Ad

1944 Coca-Cola World War II Return soldier Magazine Advertisement

Have a Coca-Cola = Howdy, Neighbor

...or greeting friends at home and abroad

Vintage 1944 Pacific Worsted Woolens Ad

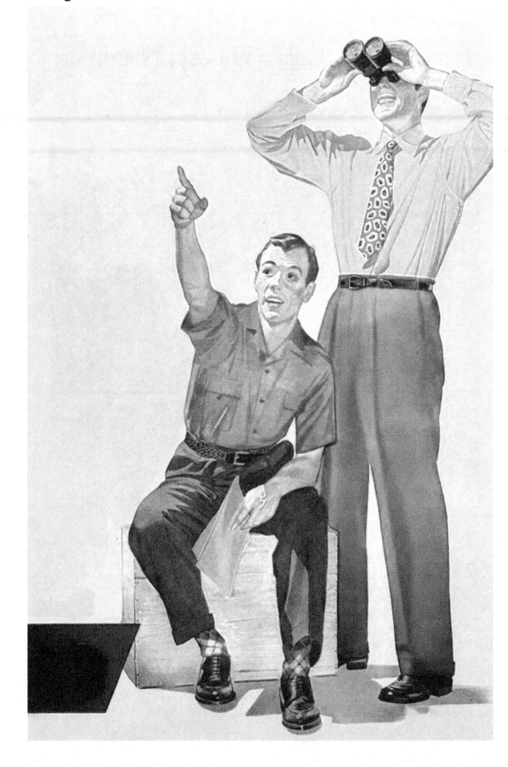

1944 Vintage ad for Wyeth`WWII era Doctor Home Visit Nurse Wheelchair Boy

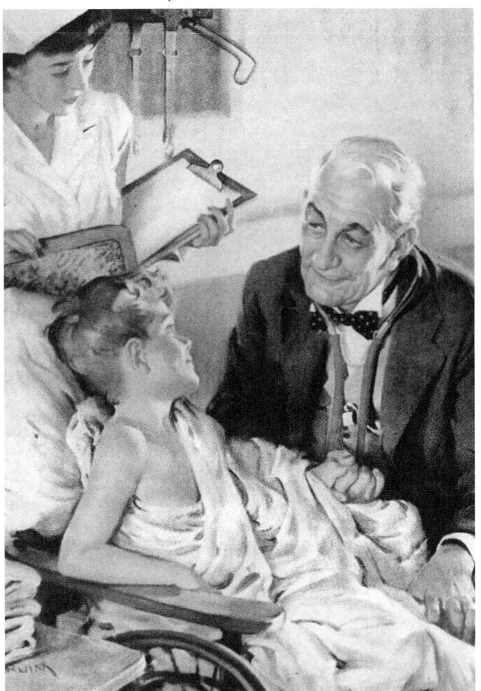

1944 vintage Budweiser print ad

1944 Snider's Old Fashioned Chili Sauce Vintage Ad

8.2 Slogans That Stood the Test of Time
U.S. Forest Service:"Only you can prevent forest fires."

Tough-yet-admirable mascot Smokey Bear starting teaching the public about wildfire prevention in 1944. The U.S. Forest Service's original slogan ("Smokey Says – Care Will Prevent 9 out of 10 Forest Fires") didn't exactly roll off the tongue, but the more memorable "Only YOU can prevent forest fires" was created a few years later. Smokey's cartoon image, which is protected by U.S. federal law, is now an endearing part of the National Park Service and is synonymous with fire safety.

Hallmark: "When you care enough to send the very best."

Hallmark started selling greeting cards in 1910. The privately held company now creates ornaments, wrapping paper, toys, and even has its own TV channel. The enduring slogan came about in 1944, illustrating the company's focus on quality and care. Hallmark cards are still popular with consumers: The greeting card giant produces 10,000 new ones each year.

8.3 Advertising trends

Advertising trends in 1944 were greatly influenced by World War II and the need to support the war effort while also catering to consumer needs. Here are some key advertising trends from that year.

Patriotic Appeals:

With the war ongoing, patriotism was a prominent theme in advertising. Many brands incorporated patriotic symbols, colors, and themes into their ads. Messages often encouraged consumers to buy war bonds, support the troops, and conserve resources.

Rationing and Conservation:

Due to rationing of essential goods like gasoline, tires, and food, advertisements frequently focused on ways to make the most of limited resources. Brands encouraged consumers to use products efficiently and reduce waste.

Women in the Workforce:

With many men serving in the military, women played a signifi‑cant role on the home front. Advertisements often depicted women working in various industries, highlighting their contri‑butions to the war effort.

Health and Nutrition:

Nutrition and health-conscious advertising gained impor‑tance during the war. Brands promoted nutritious foods and supplements to ensure that both civilians and soldiers were well-nourished.

Cigarette Ads:

Cigarette companies were major advertisers during this period, targeting both civilians and soldiers. Some brands, like Lucky Strike, emphasized their support for the troops with military-themed campaigns.

Radio Advertising:

Radio remained a dominant advertising medium. Brands sponsored popular radio shows and used jingles and catchy slogans to create memorable ads.

Technological Innovation:

While wartime production was the focus, there were still innovations in advertising techniques. The use of color printing in magazines and newspapers became more common, adding visual appeal to ads.

Activity: 1944 Advertisements Memory Game

A) Snider

B) U.S. Forest Service

C) Hallmark

D) Whitman

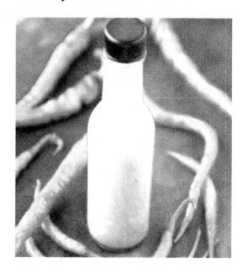

Objective: Test your memory and knowledge of 1944 advertisements by matching images or products with the corresponding brands or agencies.

This memory game allows you to engage with the advertisements of 1944 in an interactive and entertaining way, testing your knowledge of slogans and products from that era.

We have heartfelt thank-you gifts for you

As a token of our appreciation for joining us on this historical journey through 1944, we've included a set of cards and stamps inspired by the year of 1944. These cards are your canvas to capture the essence of the past. We encourage you to use them as inspiration for creating your own unique cards, sharing your perspective on the historical moments we've explored in this book. Whether it's a holiday greeting or a simple hello to a loved one, these cards are your way to connect with the history we've uncovered together.

Happy creating!

Activity Answers:

Chapter 1:
1. PARIS
2. CHURCHILL
3. DEGAULLE
4. D-DAY
5. LENINGRAD
6. ROOSEVELT
7. ICELAND
8. HITLER
9. STALIN

Chapter 2:
1. B) Double Indemnity
2. B) Bing Crosby
3. A) Judy Garland
4. A) Laura
5. A) Ingrid Bergman
6. C) Classical music performances
7. C) Variety show
8. C) Casablanca
9. A) True
10. C) Television

Chapter 3:
1. Swing, moonbeams, jar
2. seeing, old, sight
3. trolley, bell
4. Island
5. ammunition
6. myself, evenin' sky, skies
7. kiddley, ivy, kiddley

Chapter 4:
1. C
2. C
3. D
4. D
5. C
6. C
7. C
8. C
9. D
10. B

Chapter 5:

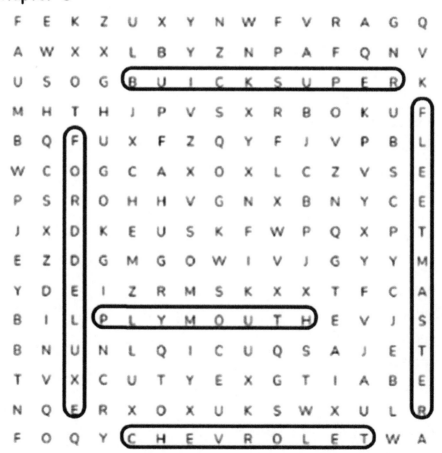

Chapter 8:

1. C
2. D
3. B
4. A

Embracing 1944: A Grateful Farewell

Thank you for joining us on this journey through a year that holds a special place in our hearts. Whether you experienced 1944 firsthand or through the pages of this book, we hope it brought you moments of joy, nostalgia, and connection to a time that will forever shine brightly in our memories.

Share Your Thoughts and Help Us Preserve History

Your support and enthusiasm for this journey mean the world to us. We invite you to share your thoughts, leave a review, and keep the spirit of '44 alive. As we conclude our adventure, we look forward to more journeys through the annals of history together. Until then, farewell and thank you for the memories.

We would like to invite you to explore more of our fantastic world by scanning the QR code below. There you can easily get free ebooks from us and receive so many surprises.

POSTCARD

Correspondence

Address

NOTE

NOTE

NOTE

TO DO LIST

- ○ --
- ○ --
- ○ --
- ○ --
- ○ --
- ○ --
- ○ --
- ○ --
- ○ --
- ○ --
- ○ --
- ○ --
- ○ --
- ○ --

well done!

TO DO LIST

- [ ] --
- [ ] --
- [ ] --
- [ ] --
- [ ] --
- [ ] --
- [ ] --
- [ ] --
- [ ] --
- [ ] --
- [ ] --
- [ ] --
- [ ] --
- [ ] --

well done!

To Do List

- [ ] _____
- [ ] _____
- [ ] _____
- [ ] _____
- [ ] _____
- [ ] _____
- [ ] _____
- [ ] _____
- [ ] _____
- [ ] _____
- [ ] _____
- [ ] _____
- [ ] _____
- [ ] _____

To Do List

- [ ] _____
- [ ] _____
- [ ] _____
- [ ] _____
- [ ] _____
- [ ] _____
- [ ] _____
- [ ] _____
- [ ] _____
- [ ] _____
- [ ] _____
- [ ] _____
- [ ] _____
- [ ] _____

Happy Birthday

note

Happy Birthday

note

Happy Birthday

note

TO DO LIST

Name: _____   Day: _____   Month: _____

No	To Do List	Yes	No

TO DO LIST

Name: _____ Day: _____ Month: _____

No	To Do List	Yes	No

NOTE

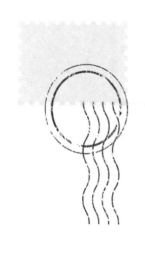

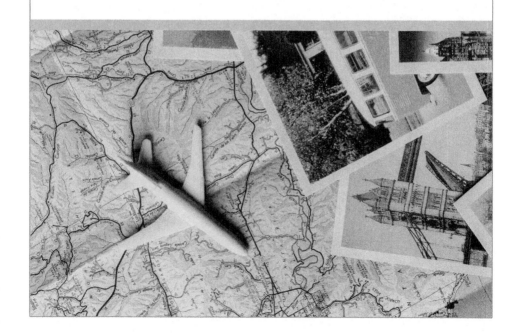

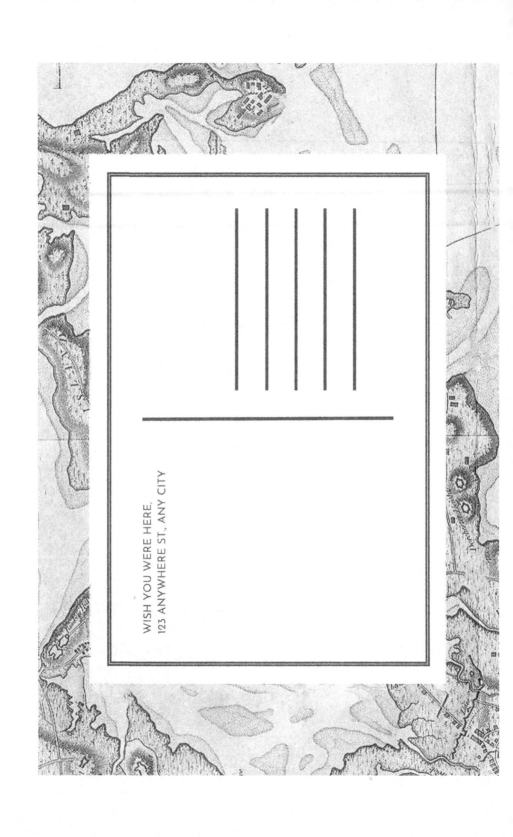

WISH YOU WERE HERE,
123 ANYWHERE ST., ANY CITY

HAPPY BIRTHDAY NOTE

TO DO LIST

Name: _____   Day: _____   Month: _____

No	To Do List	Yes	No

Remember This!

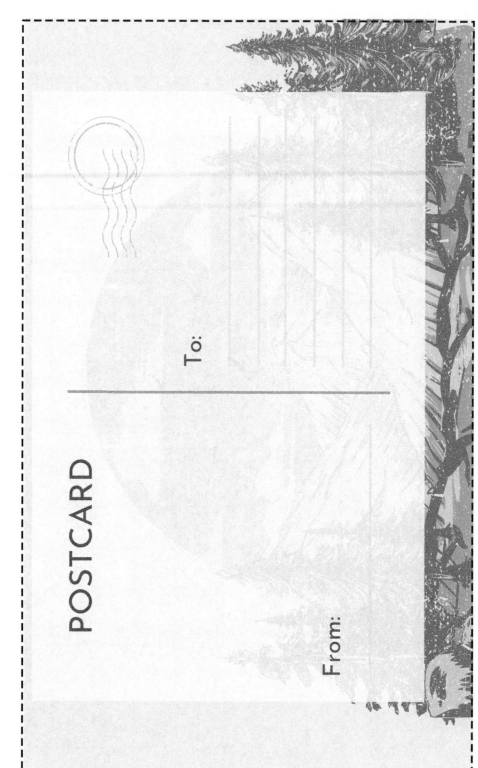

POSTCARD

To:

_____

From:

Printed in Great Britain
by Amazon

46248834R00069